E
S
S
E
N
C
E

Thuy On is an arts journalist, editor, critic and poet. She's the Reviews and Literary Editor of online publication ArtsHub. She has written two previous collections of poetry produced by UWA Publishing: *Turbulence* (2020) and *Decadence* (2022).

Images in verse are not mere decoration, but the very essence.

T. E. Hulme

The very essence of literature is the war between emotion and intellect, between life and death. When literature becomes too intellectual – when it begins to ignore the passions, the emotions – it becomes sterile, silly, and actually without substance.

Isaac Bashevis Singer

PRAISE FOR ESSENCE

Thuy On's poetry re-focuses the world. Reading *Essence* truly takes us into what is essential, distils moments, pins experience. On puts language under pressure, firing each poem into an exquisite sculpture. Building on past books *Turbulence* and *Decadence*, this collection continues to express a love affair with what words can do. There is such versatility here. From the passion and eros of the body to yearnings of the heart, from the playfulness of artistic and linguistic gymnastics to searing intellectual insights. I love spending time in On's world. The way I am bounced from sumptuous visuals to sonorous aural immersions, the way it also makes me slow down and savour. This is a poet who pays microscopic attention to detail and for whom language is at once a playground and a laboratory. Every poem owns its place, exemplifying Shakespeare's urging of brevity and wit. And yet each poem also holds larger universes. To borrow some of On's language, these poems blister, chisel and weave. This collection is ocean-hearted.
EMILIE COLLYER

Full of paeans to pop songs and cold-cut lit classics whilst taking apart the machinery of cultural criticism (and consumption), this collection also hums with a blood-red and ocean-hearted longing for connection beyond the page.
DAVID STAVANGER

At its heart, Thuy On's latest collection is a sassy critique of the world of art and literature and all of our earnest exertions in pursuit of this thing called Art. *Essence* raises fundamental questions about the labours involved, among them: the labour of creation, the labour of criticism, the ongoing emotional labour required to resist 'overripe' orientalist tropes that diminish us all. The strength of this collection lies in its adept inter-textuality, irony and reflexivity, and refusal to take itself too seriously. These are supple poems that interrogate themselves and each other, and by extension, our assumptions about poetry and literature and what we as creators and consumers collaboratively and performatively proclaim to be Art.
GRACE YEE

PRAISE FOR TURBULENCE and DECADENCE

Its compass needle searching for true norths of connection, *Turbulence* draws the reader across the affective straits of contemporary female experience. In equal parts meditative and bombastic about the human desire for intimacy, *Turbulence* explores possible passage and harbour for the self linguistically and socially. This self-aware volume navigates states of romantic, maternal, and authorial vulnerability. Just as revelatory and sometimes stark moments are accompanied by wry resilience, a neologistically rich and condensed lyricism is combined with perceptive critiques of how social media and dating apps shape both modern desire and expectations around women.
2021 MARY GILMORE AWARD JUDGES

Thuy On's *Decadence* is a thrilling and wry evisceration of poetry gate-keeping on this continent. She sometimes resists the non-poet reader, and other times brings them in openly on the joke without resorting to the easy gags about poetry. Even as it endlessly needles the industry in which it's situated, *Decadence* stands in as a kind of portfolio demonstration of On's craft and cleverness as a poet – focussed, sensual, critical, charged, interdisciplinary. As a book of poems about poems, it inevitably turns in on itself in a delicious way, but despite this *Decadence* is rarely up itself. When the collection looks outside to apply or play out its theories, On provokes us as readers to reconsider the role of poetry in our lives.
2023 STELLA PRIZE JUDGES

Melbourne critic Thuy On's debut poetry collection, *Turbulence*, is sensuous, accessible and impressive. These lyric poems, which cover the eternal verities of love and poetry in a refreshingly contemporary timbre, derive their dynamic force from an interplay of deep feeling and wit. They are quicksilver and uncluttered, playfully open yet supple and elliptical, forever zooming in and out of focus.
JAMES ANTONIOU, THE SYDNEY MORNING HERALD

To say that reading Thuy On's poetry is as if we are on that emotional rollercoaster with her is an understatement. One minute, you're excited by the prospect of new love, and the next you're aggrieved with loss. And On's gift is in being able to spark this catalogue of feeling within her readers. But the skilful way in which she can manipulate words with such vivid imagery that we can almost reach out and touch it is impressive.
JACKIE SMITH, *MASCARA LITERARY REVIEW*

Turbulence evoked a complete spectrum of emotions, a whole sum of a person provided generously and unpretentiously. There is something calming in On's almost scientific clarity and reflections. Like watching a movie on a plane, they provided me the freedom to appreciate every emotion I felt in the process.
HANEEN MAHMOOD MARTIN, *INDAILY*

Thuy On's poems are sinewy vines on which the fruit of love and loss have ripened and the resin of language is pressed in its second skin. A new voice in Australian poetry where life writing and the lyric are never too sweet, nor too dark, though often a surprising and lingering blend.
MICHELLE CAHILL

Thuy On's poetry lives in the present tense of the present moment. It's fluid, it's vibrant, and it doesn't stop talking to you the reader, for Thuy On has the rare gift of going right up to the reader and talking about anything and everything unashamedly all at once and with a voice that is smart, intelligent, alive and sensual. If it's 'a somersaulting fish in the rib cage' kind of poetry you would read (if you read poetry) then this is that kind of poetry. Thuy On has (as she says) a cynic's head and a poet's heart. These poems, heartfelt and cynical, are brief enough to operate like a speed dating experience. Each one you read might be one of the ones you want to keep around and live with for a long time. When Thuy On writes that 'Life is not for making reservations but for turning up and hoping

a table's free,' she's talking about turning up at an Anthony Bourdain restaurant, and yes, that would be one way of saying I am alive, I am here, I am hungry, and I am everything anyone could imagine a poet might be.
KEVIN BROPHY

Funny, clever and keenly observed, *Decadence* is a profound musing on literature and language, that deftly skewers the would-be gatekeepers of verse. With this second collection, Thuy On has cemented herself as a vibrant, unique and captivating new voice in Australian poetry.
MAXINE BENEBA CLARKE

In *Decadence*, Thuy On indulges in her love of language, assembling a unique erotics of word and punctuation, showcasing a poetry that is pure – in being about itself – but also powerfully seductive. As the poet herself puts it, this is 'art laid bare,' performing how language works as language but also as a window onto those dark, human mysteries of being and feeling. Indeed, if On builds such a brilliantly decadent mansion out of poetry, exploiting striking imagery and playful wit, it is ultimately to provide a kind of refuge, 'lest the cave of night swallows you.'
MARIA TAKOLANDER

Thuy On's poems are always wry, epicurean and defiant. Literate yet disarmingly unpretentious, wildly playful yet leavened with complex feeling, *Decadence* is a surreptitious delight.
ANDY JACKSON

ESSENCE

Thuy On

UWA PUBLISHING

First published in 2025 by
UWA Publishing
Crawley, Western Australia 6009
www.uwap.uwa.edu.au

UWAP is an imprint of UWA Publishing
a division of The University of Western Australia

THE UNIVERSITY OF
WESTERN
AUSTRALIA

ISBN: 978-1-76080-299-8

NATIONAL
LIBRARY
OF AUSTRALIA

A catalogue record for this
book is available from the
National Library of Australia

Cover design by Alissa Dinallo
Typeset in Joanna Nova by Lasertype
Printed by Lightning Source

❶ ⓘ ❷ uwapublishing

U W
A P **90** CELEBRATING YEARS

CONTENTS

Essence

Spend your words wisely
adjectives are a finite commodity
& you can't be a wastrel novelist
edit like a poet plying ikebana
image through shape line colour

think of waves falling like octaves
a wending river mirroring sky
a sand mandala swallowed by tide
the warming thermals of dawn
then braille read the ink pot of stars.

Art

If I were Poet Laureate: a mandate

1. Acrostics across the sky
Petrarchan sonnets on bridges
connecting lovers on opposite cities.

2. Low flying drones to drop care packages
a confetti of verses on downtrodden heads
scraps of bibliotherapy for the desolate.

3. Neon glow-in-the-dark chalk deployed
by a rag tag of street urchins
cursive beacons in the inky gloom.

4. Public transit graffitied with couplets
literal concrete poetry on worksites
ballads on bollards tankas on tonka trucks.

5. Haiku hung aloft every street lamp
elegies sung by honeyeaters with golden bells
a choral cantata to rouse the sunken.

To Maggie Cheung, In the Mood for Love

I bought a blood red
velvet cheongsam
fringed with black lace
and thought of your
slender pillar holding it all in

no spillage dare permissible
held together by knotted buttons
lily neck upright via Mandarin collar
encased in floral proprieties
softness trained to rigour

you are lowered eyes and mute lips
you are jewelled pomegranate seeds
constrained in a skin of desire
you are sashaying down stairwells
forsaking the shadow in the depths

I wore a blood red
velvet cheongsam
fringed with black lace
and thought of your
slender pillar holding it all in.

Get Lit Again (with one Aussie cameo)

While Piggy, sans glasses, is wrestling for the conch
Raskolnikov is preoccupied sharpening his axe
Kurtz is staring at the mirror, razor aloft—oh the horror!
and Boggis, Bunce and Bean are waiting in sentinel

Wilbur is doing his hardest to look radiant
Milo is confused with signposts from the Whether Man
Under and over the Eloi and Morlocks are playing catch chasey
And Lady C is forgetting who she is in the p(h)easant hut

Lucy may be skip-hopping along with Mr Tumnus
but in another galaxy Arthur is being tortured by Vogon poetry
Yossarian is clutching his belly in mock agony
and Meursault is just another word for malaise is it not?

Bertie is dashing off to find a cow-creamer what-ho!
pouting Sebastian refuses to go anywhere without Aloysius
Grenouille is on the sniff for the raw and nubile
and Ponyboy is trying to stay gold in the omniscient doom

The six characters looking in vain for their author
run into Estragon and Vladimir on the kerb
and though Willy's wares are rejected home to home
Nora's door slamming is heard the world over

Lost and dazed Murakami is once again dreaming of cats
no one cares about your fishin', huntin' and boozin' Papa H
with the housing crisis, it's now a (shared) room of your own
and seriously all of your characters need a slap Tsiolkas.

Deflation

after Death of a Salesman

Attention must
be   paid
but no one is buying you and as a small man
you're just as exhausted as a great one you
didn't go into the jungle diamonds didn't light
your way once so weighty with charisma you're
now dropping currency with seeds planted in
darkness never to be harvested the Great Dream
a deflated balloon among the football and soda
pop with past and present vision in collision look
at you in the bleachers eyes on your first born on
the green but he's not going to redeem you the
the root and branch of your life this is a modern
Greek tragedy after all so crumpled crushed by
capitalism wrapped up in candied slogans a study
in entropy unable to be saved even in death.

I don't love you any time

after *Miss Saigon*

Hey don't get mad this is not for you

you're not rich white
in velvet seats
saucer eyes waiting

for overripe tropes of war
to theatre-rise & muzak gush:
Vietnam whorehouses US helicopters

Asian women in their ao dais dancing
for saviours on the other side of the earth
(that's how they find their worth)

watch the cosseted swallow
reheated *Madama Butterfly*
staleness fishboned in their throats

loving it anyway why wouldn't they
mouth along to this paternalistic paean
plump throats thrilling to the beat

of diverse colours validation
composed by two French men
with colonialism in their blood ink

razor edged circumscribing
forever roles to the fetishised wounded
(hey ingrates at least you lot appear on stage.)

The night encroaches

after Edward Hopper's *Nighthawks*

It's 2am the fluorescent light wanly flickers
the night owls gather creeping sad

outside the streets have lost their traffic
stiff peaks of animation now flatlined

inside upon timber stools and nauseous walls
every heart a metronomic slow down

each coiled within desires unmatched
fingers tapping to ashy melodies

these half-lit faces half juttering requests
silence swallows the faltering rest.

The Walk

after The Cure

One hundred days have passed
let's rejoice at the end of an error
take my hand into a forest to play for today
lie traverse against a fallen branch
so close to me we are inbetween days
just say yes it's never enough a night like this
let's go to bed on a sheet of mossy leaves
underneath the stars in the hanging garden
catch the lullaby of the lovecats this is our lovesong.

Shocked

after Kylie Minogue

Reading the topography of your face
and I am shocked (shocked)

the blood rush to my own
I should be so lucky

to run my fingers along
your faint blue veins

once again I am shocked (shocked)
the red bright life of you

my hand on your heart
the four chambers of my own

the quiver and pulse
when you shadow near

the thrumming heat of you
such long-lashed flickers

and I am spinning around
shocked (shocked)

wishing I could step back in time
to where all the lovers breathe

to keep the inevitable at bay
so I won't be shocked (shocked)

when we're finally parted
and you stand cold as stalactite.

After Life

after *Giselle*

The Wilis are there in a circle
holding the hands of Miss Havisham
sprightly whitely they spin
round and round and round
atwirl and drop and open-mouthed
voiceless their throats full of stones

once prostrate in thirsty graves
all now rise again to bewitch
the faithless Albrechts who broke
their minds in the breathing world
dance prance with us they beckon
welcoming me in their embrace

bearing sorry tales of of my own
my silver slippered feet finding the beat
artless heartless I join their fold
such luminous exquisite corpses
and in communion with the spectral trees
we sigh cajole and wrest back control.

Golden Ratio

after Jeffrey Smart

It is *always* about the geometry
being a libertine with shapes

rules so sharp you can cut yourself
let others proselytise about blades of grass

shipping containers carry their own worth
man-made is next to Godliness

& critics can exhaust themselves:
post-industrial Orwellian doom

hyper real/surreal/classicist/formalist?
for you it's just play with maths and paint.

Nude in Recline

I want to be in a Bonnard painting
his brush to glide over
the cello of my back
fingered by the dying sun

indifferent to his strokes
face lost to the wallpaper
blushed cheeks in view
suffused in languor

I want a concert of tangerine reds
in gentle-footed duet
an emerald ombre vista
pulsing in the heat.

Ode to the critic

How unconscionable there's no statue of a critic!

[world-weary hands to sweating brow]

we're martyrs after all

in service to truth and beauty

tasked to savour and suffer the fruits of the Artz

bookworming through titles unworthy of the dead forests from whence they came

scribbling in the dark during the second Act & trying to interpret hieroglyphics in the morn

placating publicists educating editors avoiding[A-lister] actors we only bestowed two stars in their last outing

verily we've blunted our pencils with all those harrumphing squiggles in the margins

worn out our arse-kicking shoes on the red carpet

dare you call us parasitic while you try to preen your wares?

you need us to needle-prick the bloated body to release the hot air

we are culture vultures picking clean those blanched bones of industry well someone has to do it to get to the marrow to the juice of it

we are town criers throwing yay or nay slips from atop towers

we are drawbridges between intention and result

we are interpreters of the unspoken

we read between the lines

between the curtains

between your ears.

Beauty and Decay

after *Time: Rone*

Flinders Street Ballroom:

The grand dame in a state of disarray
undressed seams on shameless display
her rooms turned over by clever hands
ghostly remnants where the light lands

surfaces and crevices mottled with dust
detritus neglected to artfully rust
recycled thrifted softwared magic
a post-war poem freeze-framed static

in the golden dusk traffic muted below
we fall into sepia slipstreams of continuum flow
discrete time capsules laid out to ingest
confetti of the real and imagined flung about lest

we ever forget that life's an exhibition on show
the theatre of love and loss from the front row
the present simply palimpsests overlaid
with the patina of yesteryear's beauty and decay.

Chekhov's gun

Unexpectedly you appeared
in the first Act all sleek and poised

Later Act II
many words exchanged
many words withheld
& you disappeared
behind the drapery

leaving me to hope-wait
your return in the final third
like a blazing Chekhov's gun.

Swan Lake haiku

Forest bathing swans
gloss around a mirror-lake
enchanted maidens.

Odette and Odile
a Jungian battle
the self and the shadow.

how Ovidian
this metamorphoses tale
white cygne blackened.

midnight to daybreak
32 fouettes on pointe
Tchaikovsky in ear.

Eternity

Arthur Stace the one word poet
with copperplate script in yellow chalk
this drunkard found God

at the height of the Depression
pre-dawn beat on Sydney Streets
hid their Eternity secrets

for 35 years: time, mortality
Christ's judgement laid out neatly
sun-ravaged, rain-washed his word

prevailing to stain our souls
just follow the undulations
transient curves to evermore.

Green Destiny

after Crouching Tiger, Hidden Dragon

Oh to wield the heavy bladed sword
fencing feints as calligraphic strokes
forests trembling with mid-air jousts
a rooftop marriage of parkour and ballet

Oh to be a desert bandit on horseback
pride of warriors at your behest
leonine rags of dust across the heat
roaring victory when blade finds quarry

Oh to dive into the immortal mist
carried away by caprice and faith
pieces of your petulant heart
to be scavenged in this world and the next.

Free style poem as interpretative dance

Imagine: arms and legs akimbo
                              jutting
out at inelegant an gles
bunny hops to the pentameter beat
pirouette at any
            twirl enjambment

neck bent awkward to one side
then the other
that's a new stanza

on tiptoes now fingertips
in worshipful reach
            to the moon

back to the audience shrug
(this bit here
is impenetrable who knows what it means)

star jump for anything in *italics*
soft shoe shuffle to build momentum

Sufi whirling (for the refrain)

slow waltz to the music in your head
only you can hear so keep 'em guessing

jaunty skip slide across the floorboards
jazz hands taaaa-daaaaa
see this clever
            wordplay right here

quick now
boom tish
curtsy
a flourish end
on pointe for full stop

no one has time for an epic heroic poem.

Twelve classic texts in Haiku

The Odyssey, Homer

PTSD y'all
nymphs, cyclops, lotus-eaters...
now home to Penny!

Oedipus Rex, Sophocles

Prophecies fulfilled
intra-familial root
soz dad... oh my eyes!

Gulliver's Travels, Jonathan Swift

Size does not matter
big, small, wise or ignorant
we are all Yahoos!

Pride and Prejudice, Jane Austen

Single white female
seeks witty bachie with cash
soz, no vicars please!

Lord of the Flies, William Golding

Brawling, killing sprees
shipwrecked choirboys turn savage
even conch not spared.

Lolita, Vladimir Nabokov

A cunning linguist
on road trip to study course
of hebephilia.

The Life and Opinions of Tristram Shandy,
Gentleman, Laurence Sterne

Born in Volume III
all these pages are missing
whoops I now digress.

Tender Buttons, Gertrude Stein

Verbal cubism
word salad shredded and tossed
nipples in free fall.

Frankenstein, Mary Shelley

Quilt of living parts
goes monstering the village
just looking for love.

The Importance of Being Earnest, Oscar Wilde

Born in a handbag
Jack earnestly discovers
his real name's Ernest.

Wuthering Heights, Emily Brontë

Out there on the moors
really, his name is Heathcliff
screaming for Cathyyyyyyy!

Waiting for Godot, Samuel Beckett

He's never coming
so why are we here again?
God(0t) fucking knows!

Clair de Lune

after Paul Verlaine

The mood's in decrescendo
and with fountains in ecstasy
the day's embers have flicked out
drawing crepuscular moves
of the fleet and restless
but the sleeping birds
and the scalloped moths
are dreamstruck on Debussy
in teardropped moonlight.

Elysian Fields

after *A Streetcar Named Desire*

Oh Blanche
from Belle Reve
to motions of desire
to Elysian fields of death

entrusting yourself
to the kindness of strangers
your cracks won't be mended
by rivets of gold or silver

there is no art to suffering
the paper lantern you place
over the naked bulb
in delusional faith

you can hide the light
but truth will out
treachery sits in family
Stella's fella the torch.

Still not a Prince

after *Beauty and the Beast*

Imagine:
the fall of the last petal

she kisses the beast
too late

a tear —
the salt of human hope

down her quizzical face
unbidden

his mind's furniture
rearranged

heart now in bloom
taking pride of place

yet still fanged and hirsute
his pulse beat strong

what would Belle do?

of course this fracture
would never be

beauty must touch beauty
inside to match surface

pretty privilege is real
in the pink of rom coms

from milk to dentures
these fairy floss tales

stick to your teeth.

If rejection slips were honest

Dear writer, thank you for submitting your manuscript to our small but plucky publishing house. After careful consideration from our ferociously hardworking editorial team we have decided not to take it further. We appreciate the time it took to craft what you believe is a work of staggering genius and we know you will see yourself reflected in your mirror of tears as a monumental loser. We know. But we don't have energy, the staff, the wherewithal, the funds, to actually care.

Dear writer, your social media following is negligible, your face doesn't have the requisite photogenic attributes that will, Helen-like, launch a thousand moveable units. You lack both the currency of youth and the mystique of a childhood trauma – nothing nasty was hiding in your woodshed.

Dear writer, frankly, your brand needs polishing and we don't the resources to sheen it. At our acquisitions meeting your work did not fall into that coveted space, the intersection between Venn Diagrams: Need and Want.

Dear writer, we're sorry but we can't give individual feedback on manuscripts proffered, suffice to say we realised a chapter in that it wasn't a gutsy crime fiction set in a small rural town starring a substance-abusing former cop who's back to settle a debt, hook up with his childhood darling and find redemption. So we stopped reading.

Dear writer, anyhoo best of luck with sending your work elsewhere. Now that we've rejected you wholesale we just hope your words don't inadvertently become published by one of our competitors and end up fooling judges and winning awards. We'd looked like a bag of dicks then.

Heart

Unable to speak I will write on your body

..

._..

_ _ _

..._

.

_._ _

_ _ _

.._

Metaverse

What if we'd met before we met
a splintered line bent in time
before the blooming of such bruises
tender-touched and under skin

        What if we'd met before we met
        crossfired in space's latticed holding
        before the dereliction of sacred duty:
        the long ambush the slog of penitence

What if we'd met before we met
a warp and weft in continuum asunder
before the palm closed tight to fist
an arrow shot wildly lain to rest

        What if we'd met before we met
        a road forsaken another enticing
        before the rush of choices derailed
        pinned us both to the one mistaken

What if we'd met before we met
an arrest of what had duly passed
before your darkness before my breakage
the rent in fabric spread smooth before us.

        galaxies would've floated in our eyes
        possibilities strung across the metaverse
        festooned like fairy lights aglow in wonder
        had stars exploded and we'd met before we met.

How to Grow a Shell

1. First take a man
lie him down starfished
eyes towards the sun

let the bite of wind
the tongue of rain
tenderise his body

the tread of ants trail
across every surface
let him kiss the void

skin and air indivisible
permeable to every
wrinkle in the earth

2. Let calluses encrust
across his heart and lungs
every beat every breath

assuaged to the rhythm
of forgiveness and care
to the past to the desiccated

only then will chemical romance:
proteins, calcium, minerals
inveigle the nervous system

harden over the softness
roll him in gentle coils
armour his precious core.

Dorian

I call you Dorian
because beauty
grace and sensitivity
ripple over the surface

but all the elements
that dance roil
beneath the smooth
conspire to undo you

I call you Dorian
because your real name
is cut from familiar cloth
you are too uncommon

tear dripped tender ache
your bearing a question mark
keeled over to nihilism
wildly grasping for purchase

I call you Dorian
because I want that portrait
shredded from neck to navel
dagger-hearted so the truth of you

can rise from the ruins
kneel crawl to stand
and I'll be there waiting
to breathe you back to life.

Come Rain or Come Shine

1. Keening at the wait
the sharp angles of you
rise above the parapet

your presence beckons
I lean into you:
a scaffolding that trembles

2. I can't give you cinders
but a wildfire
searing across the copse

I don't do small
my gestures are ocean-hearted
a waterfall to fill your cup.

Saturday

There will be nothing
outside this room
beyond this bed

the moat around us
can be ringed with fire
let the world burn

there is only skin
osmotic in feeling
rippling in tune

so tell me of the labyrinth
coiled inside you
in the shrouded light

your eyelashes alone
their rapid beckoning
will turn tides in me

we can wax and wane
cortex flooded with
moonshine and wine.

Sensitivity Reading

When I let my lips wander
open then close
parts of you in my mouth
it's a sensitivity reading

give yourself over to me
glide and ride and
learn the alphabet of my body
conjugate me verbally

I want to crawl
into the cubbyhole of your heart
each breath like moth wings
flutter soft against me

a tremor transcribed
with the deftness of tips
an intra-cultural exchange
your surrender my pleasure.

Animal antics

When the monkey meets the rat
there'll be the making of mischief and merry

cheek and bluster on your name card
precariously balanced means further to fall

tempered by my nose to the ground
dispensing earthy directives to survive

both of us fire signs lion and archer
in restful truce there's no prey no hunter

just a slow burn a cosmic pairing
a steady flame to shame all others.

Vis-à-vis

Your face is an ornament
precious to touch
moulded by striving
brooding in repose

your face can whet desire
launch a chorus of songbirds
break time's millstone
lead still waters to shiver

your face reflects and refracts
shards glued together
a minutiae of regrets
glimmering in the dust

your face hides softness
flash storms in the dark
a Cubist glamour of angles
a provocation that hurts.

Room 1101

The world below
is a Pissarro smudge

behold our mirror double
strike that pose darling

are we not delicious models
in this moment of pause?

your legs vined around me
a study in charcoal

and decadent space
in the dust of lowlight

apricity beyond these walls
beckon the return of public

but we are not ready yet
the weather here is peach

enough with breath
waves across the sheets

bedwrecked and spent
we list side to side

drowning finally
to the siren of sleep.

Version 2.0

I want to re-write you
so you're ablaze within
by tiny refracted red suns
and vertically stretched rhizomes
can pull at your nervous system

I want to re-write you
raise you from the catacombs
home you inside a shooting spaceship
drive you through midnight arteries
so swift your breath mists

I want to re-write you
lean my weight against the wrecking ball
wrap you in an infinity scarf
absorb your meld of data and cells
hyperlink them to my fingerprint.

Memento Vivere

I love you like Icarus loved the sun
scorched wingtips flailing for purchase
this vertical blaze shooting true north
with swoop of ribcage exposed and ashen

When the day waned I loved you still
the air heavy with heat and remembrance
memento vivere an incantation on my lips
when faltering as the light guttered and died
and took you captive to the thrall of chance.

Revenant

I ignored the sign
hung askew over your breastbone:
please don't feed this heart

but my own yearned and burned
biopsy of delusion
breath ripping like wet tissue

now unpicking the threads of us
sky sewn in tattered drapes
I am still vulnerable

to ghost nights unexorcised
revenant in my dreams
seething and grasping

we rode the line
until the sentence ended
this is the part where I leave you

cut the strings looping
the pearls of us to slacken
slip in the sibilance of rain.

Whirligig Days

I thought you were exotic
       our connection madly erotic
but it turned out you were neurotic
       our love is now historic
whirligig days were chaotic
       nights of stone left me moronic

this empty page is a buoy
to be filled with words
that will leak over the sides
an oversplash
of non-curation
best shut your eyes
stop the tidal wave

this is hardcore
this is closed door
this is time whore
this is iron claw
this is mental chore
this is body store
this is rough raw
this is never more.

Trompe l'oeil

With you I was silvery lambent
then you passed through like mist
now stripped of effulgence
memories breaking under my ribs
I'm a trompe l'oeil
only from a distance
do the pieces hold up.

Why you should not break a poet's heart

We may look soft and squishy
on our diet of daffodils and clouds
pallid and dim from adoring moonshine

we moth-bitten outcasts of industry
limbs draped loosely on chaise lounges
as we swoon and try to grasp the ineffable

but with a single stroke from our limp wrist
we can eviscerate peace evermore
call on the spirits of Poe and Shelley

to parry and thrust at your sleep
and that twist in your entrails?
that's our voodoo words at play

the curse of a poet is as potent as fire
we'll write you in red ink small font
throw your halo to the blistering pyre.

Sunny side up

The sun cracked like an egg on the tin roof
& we stood under the warmth of its yolk
the viscosity of that day coated me

an age waiting for the season to mellow
for the maple to burst to flame
right down to its blackened bones

once I dripped fed you the sea
breathed the air of your lungs
an odalisque painted by your eye

we were Broadway choreography
the rapture of synchronicity
now a solo dance an erratic beat

I remind myself you are just one star
not the cosmos your influence finite
I can square up to other futures.

Exeunt

This story could not load
please check your connection and try again
if the problem persists consider refreshing the page

oh we know what the issue is
you have too many browsers open
too many fucking choices

you can't just open and close one
but keep a history of hurts
and potentials to flick through

the reels have flashed by
highlights in technicolour
now on the cutting room floor

you: tower-high enforced by bramble
me: no longer slashing through thicket
neither of us are out of the woods

this story is going to self-destruct
these *sites de memoire* will implode
please strap yourself in before countdown.

Cadence

It's nearly Spring but trees are only half dressed/night anoints
the moon with its milky full belly/ restlessness beats on the
footpath/a rogue rainbow already gone to prism/a light sentence
that gives it time to reflect

in the distance the architecture of you /looms preternaturally a
column exposed/to weathered skies/tidepools of your eyes greeny
blue/shadowed over

composed of relics/mismatched particles of history/you are what
you were/self made/undone/ stitches unwound in time/disturbed
from its moorings/to me as handsome as propaganda

susurration of your greetings stirs me/later/the diaphanous
morning now opaque/I want to be intimate with the texture of
your days/read the goosebumps stippled on your skin/count the
xylophone of jutted ribs/play you pianissimo.

Thief

What does it mean to steal a kiss?
was it secreted within spidery coves

do you follow the footfalls in the gloom?
was it hidden in the splash of pebbles

stuck like Gymea lilies in highway concrete?
can the task to find it be slipped in

between the errands of pearl-grey pigeons
wheeling in hungry arcs over skylines?

I need to capture map it zoom in close
from suburb to street to bedroom window

to sheets as frenzied as a rip current
to see upon the pillow the gift of your lips.

Seduction (2 stars)

He is neatly combed as a zen garden
lemon-scented trying to impress
so she can unbutton her skin to him
expose the very bosom of her wants

beneath the impenetrable night he needs
her awaken by his hand alone
but tasked to regurgitate dictionaries
declaim in shades of violet prose

he is all thumbs no mouth
dazzled by her dust jacket
extrinsics he feigns sudden dyslexia
their story stops & she remains unproofed.

Rehab

So apparently I foster men
til they find their forever homes
after being de-barked, socialised
tutored in different settings
now pliant of pleasant mien
ready to be petted by other hands

with enormous appetites
they will yes, eat you out
lick their appreciation every which way
til strange random smells seduce
& they follow heavy balled
blue tongue lolling.

La Dolce Vita

My polyglot
with his clever tongue
slicks it in
before in boxing me
that ache of contact
fingers in my mouth
damming the vowels
my polyglot
with his Romance
languages all the sounds
that end in o
coming together
an aria in the dimlight.

Beasts

A room in heat
penumbra framed
I can't see your blue
just half lidded apertures
blinking in rasps
in this hour of frantic
where we stop cosplaying humans
and strip to the animal.

Scene 3. Late night

I'm sorry for everyone who's not us/ drizzle dark outside/silvered
fresh/curlicues of voices beyond/on your bed/a current from
tip to tip/burnished hard and bright/sweet salty/dirty clean/
yearnings that make my heart hot/communion of expectation &
satiation/a wanderlust fathomless/ the entire world here/neither
drunk/but we are inebriated/I am thirsty for you/I wear your
amorous dreams over my body/the moon-pale of yours/in beat/
in chorus/being with you/is like taming the sun/slipstreams of
radiance/haloing me/ I shine.

Touchstone

With the point chisel
I chip out these words

their nacreous gleam
in the exhalation of night

pearls that trickle
in open palms:

golden brown
salt of your skin

your surf-flecked
birth town writ tall

curve of clavicle
press of pelvis

naked of neck
mythology of muscles

Michelangelo's
marbled angel

set free.

Resolutions

I'd like to string stories
of multi-coloured beads

I'd like to scribble poems
as smoke signals in the sky

I'd like to dream us
on Pegasus against the ivory dawn

I'd like to perch
in a lighthouse to scorn wrecks

I'd like to wish
on an archipelago of stars

I'd like to revivify
with flaming trees

I'd like to spin
to the jazz of your voice

I'd like to be gluttonous
on your skin

Come climb these
trellises of veins
to a face of berry stains
and kohl

Let us be

food

church

anchor

heat.

(A)part

Apart

A part

of my heart

        is parboiled in syrup

        bruised purply raw taste of iron

emotions are cartoons

        anvil migraine of colours

        thought bubbles bursting

and the clocks go forward tonight
as they do every night
and I am still where I am

nights of unpunctuated prose
committing crimes against grammar
quondam dreams in seams

negative space between my ribs
coordinates misplaced
mute in dialects of loss

black hole swallowed whole
I will no longer
move tongue and muscle over you

the fallen of crest
the begone of woe
the storming of brain
the shocks of after
the stricken of love.

Plot Twist

You've stopped turning the page
to bask in your own fiction
an errant fool who left the stage

forgotten the rose of beginning
incapable of seizing my worth
you've stopped turning the page

an actor who never missed a cue
all lines delivered in perfect play
an errant fool who left the stage

once the architect of my days
blueprint now in disarray
you've stopped turning the page

spinning me to a dervish grief
creator of this bloody revolution
an errant fool who left the stage.

Send in the Clown

In media res here he comes
dropped from a chary universe

weary of her tears
here: have a clown

he is: sans red nose
he has: average shoes

he has: thick floofy hair
he is: long-limbed grins

a wandering star
to her fixed point

on loan for a spell
lost in her city

to beguile smiles
to charm disarm

a one-man festival
a one-woman audience

such a limited season
exclusive to her only

then a bow a scatter of claps
his lips imprinted on hers

and with a tricksy finale
he disappears into air.

Tears for a Clown

Fitful, he wakes in the dark
in his knapsack; his shell
he carries his home:

clothes, laptop, room
for kindness nestled
in the hidden fold

an edict: no long farewell
a showman, but nothing public
masks are his third language

she's soft-toe quiet
letting her emotions sleep in
knowing the path

of divergence will unease
when fully roused
so she tarries a beat

then: a small embrace
she holds herself still
waits til the door shuts

and as the world spins
returns to the unmade bed
blinks at the encroaching light.

Jouissance

1. Time is freshening
you are still so new

to be read through fingertips
kisses as extraction of knowledge

books, cats, plants
this trifecta a hyphen between us

and the lusciousness of words
you also carve and relish

an impresario's tableau
of civilised-hungry

2. The swell, rise, release
only a partial understanding

it's the quintessence of you
an orb-weaver web

finely spun complexity
to be parsed and grasped

strand by golden strand
awaiting illumination

but first let's commit
to the taste of ordinary ecstasies.

A chapter in

If only you'd drunk
more deeply from this flower
crossed the bridge
over language's chasm

If only you'd realised
I didn't want to carry the weight
of another life but to touch it:

break through threads of sunlight
write in the cells of memory
agitate for verses and music

but now a fallow stillness
and these bruises will turn pale
as once upon a time frescoes.

13 ways of looking at love

1. It's a truth universally acknowledged that a love that can start wars, inspire art and spark revolutions will never begin with, 'Hey, pretty lady'.

2. Licking the taste of recklessness will spark electrons in the air.

3. A cherry-lipped hurt will follow monasteries of silence.

4. Billie Holiday's pristine gardenias hid a scorched undergrowth.

5. Being a slave to a cat is still better than being a doormat of a man.

6. Drinking a vial of men's tears is only momentarily satisfying.

7. The fourth finger of the left hand does not contain a vein leading to the heart.

8. It's not our ability to love that makes us human; it's actually our ability to select each image containing traffic lights.

9. You can be soft edged and lucent by candle or lit by the filigrees of stars.

10. Your fingers dancing over me are wild birds in flight.

11. Dating apps inflict the worse pain imaginable.

12. Sometimes it really isn't love but limerence.

13. Blackbird against snow: my hair on your pillow.

À la carte

WA Sunsets

Eat me already
peaches, persimmons blush ripe
stickiness of heat.

Tulip

How deep-throated and operatic you are
extroverting after adoration and how we oblige
angling you for the best light all the better
to admire such post-show party decolletage

how you fling yourself wildly to the sun
desperate for validation only a few days
before wrinkled debauchery claims

the breast you once vaunted so brazenly
the blush the swoon the droop the fall
a Monet melodrama in four exquisite Acts.

Natural violence

In the southern tinderbox
after a bushfire sunset:

chiaroscuro of earth and sky
flamboyant Nureyev flame-leaps

as the earth trudged on its axis
cicadas in their carapaces boiled

snapdragons' fists charred closed
and a scimitar-bladed moon melted.

Someone once said a burial
looks like a planting:
it's not a death but a renewal

but unbeknown to me
we were tents in a blizzard
stones rolling underfoot

with the wild leaves outside
calligraphic portents
swirling dust motes.

51 Shades of Green

What a lungful
this collective of green
baby shoots to old growth
the moss velvet
the cool bracing
the scent of living

with straighter backs
we bathed in *komorebi*
sluiced the dampness
over city husks
can you feel us germinating
pushing tired bones to air?

Bold Type

We Helveticas are everywhere
down subways across shopping centres
hey heyyying on dating apps

s(t)olid pillars
tempting you into our cult
be like us we can give you

unencumbered lines
soft smooth curves
respectability & ineffability

none of those serif riff-raffs
uncouth fringe-dwellers
taking all sorts of liberties

protective membranes
that will hold you together
we are the ruling classes.

FANBOYS mnemonic

for and nor but or yet so
come stick with us conjunctions
we work hard we connect and coordinate
important clause to *important clause*
even though we are always passed over
for promotion unlike those (wily)adjectives
and adverbs (sneakily) making themselves
indispensable to every poet's toolkit
we too deserve to be fanboyed over.

Contronym

You

bolt: secure/fleeing
bound: tied up/desirous of escape
inflammable: on fire/immuned to rage

moving from the cool blues
to Holly Golightly's mean reds
unsettled and shaken like a snow globe

essayer is French for 'to try'
verily you are an essay
so trying.

Breathe

Left and right atrium
left and right ventricle

the punctuation of breaths
arrhythmic beats

bruised as a Caravaggio apple
softly plump flesh sallow sweet

breathe

glow slow like Rothko's panels
stake your form in space

whip off those cumulus sheets
swallow bathe in delicious colour

breathe.

Parachute

You think this sentence is ready to die but no not yet there may
be a comma or a semicolon or even an em dash reprieve with
more life to come so just wait it out I know the rock between
your shoulder blades is impossibly heavy the tears of acid
peeling your face to bone & you've held misery like a newborn
to the chest shrapnels of memory under your skin you've been
impersonating yourself emoting the loneliness of a marathon
runner fighting for scraps of love like a pigeon watching the
world turn through a cloud of cataract stagger drunk on acedia
so time now to rest your head red wine heavy between my hip
and ribs your neck so exposed and fragile think of the knobbles
of your spine as stepping stones exalt in larks like choirboys
spin a new language with your fingers unclench your fist
notice how the night falls on our heads like an ombre silk veil
navy indigo prussian obsidian draw aside the curtain of trees
photosympathise with plants admire the geometric perfection of
ferns grace the parachute blossoming above.

To be a perfomative Asian

Hey banana   we need to peel you

there's whiteness in the corner of your eyes
whiteness if you care to b(l)end and genuflect

POC – meaning whiteness a default
normcore against which you are measured

are you eggshell-coloured, ecru, dove-grey?
all those smudgy off-white tones

tell us at least you are trying
to mitigate against your yellowface

will you change your name for us?
our tongues cannot twist that much

our fulsome thanks to those
who understand the need to heed

that a protruding nail will get hammered
better then to be model minority

go polish your mannequin limbs
& we'll hoist you up to the bamboo ceiling.

Fake Asian

Spitting out my filial piety with the beef offal congee
I sharpened my chopsticks against the grain
ran wild with young white boys on campus
majored in the belles-lettres of old white men
minored in contrary and rebellion
graduated with Honours in make believe

a robe of insouciance slipped over my shoulders
I play acted in a stage of my own creation
when all the real Asians married dentists
and traded Monopoly investment houses
and cooked three hour broth with ginseng
and made their kids regurgitate chords and numbers.

The Game of Life

I have too many vowels
you have too many consonants

surely we cannot continue like this
such random falls from the sky

bereft of meaning I am waiting
for that elusive blank slate

I need to score quickly
a hit twice and thrice

one can do so much with so little
just a matter of place setting

it's all about location
location location

like a poem distilled
into trace elements

yet still holds power
the pieces in your palm.

Lost in IKEA

I reckon we've passed that Kivik three times remember that sage or is it khaki ottoman on the right of the Liatorp that everyone covets and the dumpy lumpy Parup found in all the share houses that ever existed we need to double up back trace to the beginning near the stegasaurus plushies bypass the fine pine ensemble of Jokkmokks again and all the Bissas and the Tjusigs and just follow the arrows and the numbered signs how hard can it be we are here aren't we but no we are supposed to be there where the rugs are where is number 16 why are we still on number 8 we have seen that Pinnig four fucking times now and I still don't want it in any of its colours it's clearly mocking us with its sturdy lines that will never take less than six hours to assemble how long have we been here already wait is that a shortcut or a trap labyrinth if we follow it will we find the cocktail glasses or will we be taken back to Linnmon and the Lagkapten once again goddam this Borgesian nightmare I knew we should have eaten the meatballs first.

Liminal

for Ava

You are now 16
the string between us
a little more slack

room to skip around its loose
knots fashion your own bows
slip over the fraying edges

your bedroom door
sometimes closed sometimes ajar
small beeps from screen

or music unknown to me
a tinny escape through headphones
bug-like in your interiority

you are an onion skin of layers
your translucence hidden
the core that once beat within me

a waif weighed down
by Dr. Martens-shod feet
shifting between liminal states

you veer in and out of focus
the child forever to me
restless to colour in

the contours of tomorrow
and I will slowly dim
as you become illuminated.

To Mochi

How fluid you are my familiar
a loaf a sphere a comet across the room

every other day it's just the two of us
black and white shadow

object d'art as glossy as pride
keeping your own counsel

with Bastet slinking in your genes
regality is conceived in your bearing

the way you invite touch
is therapy incarnate

marble eyes shut weapons sheathed
rumbling motor on idle.

Blackheads

Yellow peril is spreading
blackheads across the white face
difficult to exfoliate stubborn grit
can you smell the tiger balm?
we are infiltrating smashing down
gates hoarded by keepers of industry
one splinter at a time.

Fall

There are twigs and leaves in our hair
scratch-crunchy carpet beneath

a hilly ascent watchtower above
splayed exposed, comma curled

we are affixed to this earth
soft bellied mammals in repose

with the air gentle to touch
smiling at the spurs of mortality

this death-tinged foliage sweeping
debris from a blue rinsed sky

we see only through half eyes
shaded, eclipsed in heat of day

layers shed already in pink skin
anticipation of burrowed play.

White Noise

Siri turn off my feelings
draw the blinds
file down the pointed sharp

that keeps me in tune
like an antenna
to all the frequencies

turn on whisper mode
deadlock the door
inter me in darkness

put me on numb mute
override the blinking cursors
reboot the CMS

close all the tabs
remove the bookmarks
activate holiday mode

soft belly prod me
tick the box that confirms
I am not a robot

Siri close me down
can you hear the
whirring agitations

an engine on speed dial
giving too much
to the ravenous?

white noise and padded cell me
the colours are too loud
I am feverish.

Heat and Haiku

The blossoming trees
spill like burst capillaries
grass bleeding crimson

Five darkly smudged arms
the chariot-wheeled starfish
brined in evening salt

Persimmons: hard orbs
of orange suns ripening
drip-melt on bluestone

Low-plucked strings moaning
through tessellated branches
startling currawongs

Beneath the sternum
such adamantine lustre
more bony than heart.

Seasonal writers

We're poets of course our favourite season is Autumn (Keats is right) a stanza in and we're ankle deep in mulch crunch leaf squinting in the creeping mist fingerless gloves poking under logs for meaning oh we are scavengers for any dropped phrase fallen from careless whispers so we can quilt them into something new.

leave Summer to the novelists let them crisp their prose, half bake them in seaweedy brine of expositions so enervating this desire to push their characters in different currents oh why is there always someone caught in the rip?

Winter? Oh the non-fiction cabal with their indexes footnotes superscripts drying on the rack inside so soggy after over-exertion you need to put a blankie over their knees they are too shivery with the shock-thrills of discovery.

Spring for all the purveyor of young 'uns the questing buds tumble of animal rhymes and lessons and crumbs from tongue-tied babes the birth of hope death of cynicism sliding down that rainbow they'll grow up soon enough just let them believe in evergreen for now.

CasE SenSITivE

Who are you really? what's your favourite colour? Your mother's maiden name? The address of the dusty house you first rolled down on your brand new red tricycle you are being toO SEnsitivE of course we are not harvesting this information it's safe you're safe you can trust us do you want your squishy insides to be hacked? you want to be authenticated right? many factors worth of verification needed so give us your mobile digits your email to synchronise the soul of your first born 8 letters 2 numbers one & and #* in there somewhere and the tricky ^ one too don't forget it's CasE SenSITive it's not our fault you only have one child and one pet you've used their names already natch still single so no sweetheart initials for you what about your favourite book character have you used Darcy before add the $$$ to remind you what Lizzy saw in him you're just as insecure as your password as unstable like this connection and will just go with the same PIN for everything now well until the next month when the whole thing starts all over again.

Herstory

The first person pronoun
so ramrod in bearing

mistress of her domain
with main character energy

she harvests the richness
of all honeycombed emotions

succubus-like
struts, purrs, inveigles

from the tower of Babel
unblinking in the storm

multi-tongued in the hubbub
ferocious in this world.

Here one moment

Sprinklers spraying on the lawn
spirograph pattern wetly

nearby the sulphurous
wattle-flames are extinguished

and the grey-rose galahs sit
unruffled as Buddha

while the chrysanthemum tea cools
in my hand the leaves swirling

in the floral china cup
on this wing-shimmer moment

let's leave the other side of daylight
brooding for another time.

Sonder

Sonder (n). The realisation that each person is living a life as vivid and complex as your own.

each of us hero, supporting cast member and stranger in random overlapping stories

your right elbow may be in their frame for a second as they wait for their espresso double shot

an extra idling by as they carry on starring in their own drama, with an unheard soundtrack: Gothic dirges to K-pop sugar

maybe you are twenty steps removed linked by a cloying invisible web

perhaps if you are a poet your private little musings will travel through the knottiness of time and space and unravel at the astonished and bemused feet of someone not expecting the stirrings of empathy to pull at them.

and with a quizzical brow furrow they think

sonder.

Pinball

Heed the soundbites of the Stoics
be caretaker of the moment
imagine the sun
is specks away from annihilation

don't be dependent clauses
but creatures of indifference
agents of your own reckoning
nature will take its cadenced course

after all the universe is change
we are but hurtling atoms
assembled then broken anew
and the future is a fiction.

Acknowledgements

Once again, thanks to everyone at UWA Publishing for believing in me; I never thought I would even have one book of poetry published let alone a third collection released.

Thanks also to my friends and family; there are just too many of you to list that I am fearful I will accidentally miss someone and will be duly guilt-stricken. But you've all been there when I needed you and I am sincerely grateful for your time, company and counsel.

Special gratitude to my dearest daughter Ava(bug) and cat Mochi.

'13 ways to look at love' was first published in *Australian Poetry Journal* 13.2
'Bold Type', 'Lost in IKEA' and 'Saturday' were first published in *Eureka Street*
'Version 2.0' was first published in *Australian Poetry Journal* 13.1
'Tulip' was first published in *Meanjin* Winter 2024
'Shocked' was first published in *Spinning Around: The Kylie Playlist* (2024)
'White Noise' was first published in *Australian Poetry Anthology* Volume 11, 2024